The Briar Patch Philosopher

John E. Phillips

The Briar Patch Philosopher

The Briar Patch Philosopher

In the briar patch of life, where the thorns grow is where you find courage, endurance, patience, faith and wisdom.

Even the good will of a bad dog is worth something. We all face bad dogs from time to time - in our work place, in our families and with our friends. Can you get the good will of that bad dog on your side?

How wealthy are you? Wealth can often be calculated by the number of people you truly trust to give you good advice.

Suffering leads to patience, patience leads to perseverance, perseverance leads to character, character leads to strength, strength leads to courage, and courage produces a happy life.

Deprive the strong, and you make them stronger. Give to the weak, and you make them weaker. The more problems we learn to overcome, the better we'll be at problem solving and decision making, and the wealthier and happier we'll be. By giving to the weak, we encourage them to be dependent and to feel entitled.

Sitting in a dungeon in England awaiting torture and death, William Wallace "Braveheart" was approached by the queen and offered poison to end his life and avoid torture. Wallace said, "Every man dies, but not every man really lives." Most people exist. Few people truly live and become what they've always dreamed of being. What are you meant to be, or what are you meant to do? If you know the answer to this question, you can truly live.

If you're wondering what's left behind when a person dies, the good that was in the man or woman continues in the ones they loved. The bad that is in a person is quickly forgotten. How much good are you leaving behind?

10 Secrets to Life

I can't do anything about others except try not to irritate them.

I can't do anything about my future, except what I do today.

I always can remember a day that was worse than today; that means today is not nearly as bad as I thought.

My situation will get better as long as I try harder today, than yesterday.

I am the only person who can make me happy or sad, and I will not give that right to anyone else.

I can solve any problem; some just take longer than others.

Education is my ticket out. The more education I get, and the faster I get it, the quicker I get out of poverty.

Work is the secret to my financial future. The more I do, the more I have.

Sleep is my enemy. The less I do it, the more I can have.

There is no problem that I will have, that my mentor can't show me how to get out of and that I can't overcome.

Thoughts on Children

One of the greatest tragedies of life is we have to wait for our children to have children of their own before they realize why we did what we did, when we did it to them when they were younger.

Every kid needs the advantage of growing-up poor. One of the biggest misconceptions in our society is: "I don't want my kids to have it as bad as I did." Growing up poor teaches great lessons and makes a youngster strong. Life is not fair!! All you have to do to survive is to do the right thing. More importantly, teach this truism to your children.

Never grow up! You don't have to. I don't plan to. If I do grow up, then death isn't far away.

***

If you aren't spanking your child when he does wrong, you're creating a monster with whom other people will have to live.

***

From the time children are born until they're 4-years old, they're not really people. From ages 4-12, they're fun. From ages 12 to 21, they know everything there is in the world to know, and they think you know nothing. From age 21 to the grave, they begin to learn just how much they don't know, and how much you do know.

***

If it's not worth a spanking, it's probably not worth doing.

Thoughts on Children

You pay for your raising when you raise a child of your own.

By helping a child, you build a family and a nation.

A good parent will interfere and have an influence in his child's life. A bad parent won't.

As a parent, you don't have to be popular - you just have to be right.

Children don't know what's best for them - but you must.

The lioness that loves her cub slaps the cub up side the head with a loving paw to teach the lessons of life properly.

Training children is like training a good birddog. You must know when to apply the rod of correction and when to apply the loving hand of praise. Too much of either will ruin the dog or the child.

The strongest fledglings are pushed out of the nest first, and the weakest birds stay the longest.

Humans are the only animals who still feed their young after they leave the nest.

~~~~~~~~~~~~~~~~~~~~

The most-important investment in life is your children - not the money you give them, but the amount of time and the value system you give them.

~~~~~~~~~~~~~~~~~~~~

If your child has to have an immediate answer, the correct answer is always "No." When you say no, nothing in your world or his world changes. When you say "Yes," the horse is out of the barn. The chances of changing a yes to a no is almost impossible. The best answer is always "Let me think about it." If the child says, "I've got to know right now," the best answer is "No." If you have a chance to think about the question the child has asked and decide what's best for you and what's best for the child, you'll make better decisions.

~~~~~~~~~~~~~~~~~~~~

Even the eagle will throw its chicks out of the nest when it's time for them to fly. Do you have any chicks in your nest that need to learn to fly on their own? If you don't throw them out of the nest, you've crippled them.

Thoughts on Courage

In the midst of danger, a courageous man finds peace and safety.

The difference between courage and cowardice is often the amount of time one has to think before acting.

Courage is only built by confronting fear.

Build the courage to charge hell with nothing but a water pistol and a good idea or a just conviction.

Courage comes when we learn a truth about ourselves, face that truth and change our lives.

Danger brings opportunity to the courageous.

Thoughts on God and Life

There are only three securities in life - your relationship with the Good Lord, what you can do with your hands, and what you can do with your mind.

No one else is responsible for the world you live in, because you have the power to change your situation and your life.

No one is a slave. If you don't like your life - change it!

Some things are worth doing just because they are the right things to do.

Even a gambler knows that heaven and hell are sure bets.

Each player deals his own hand to win or lose.

God's train always runs on time. The problem most of us have is we don't know His schedule.

I know I'm burning the candle at both ends. All I need is a little more wax for the middle.

I don't want the candle of my life to burn low and then finally go out. I want to burn my candle as bright and as high for as long as it will. When that light goes out, let it go out shining brightly.

⊱─────❀─────⊰

If all the problems in the world were dumped on the courthouse steps, you'd fight to keep your own.

⊱─────❀─────⊰

There are always two answers to any problem - the emotional and the factual. Bet on the facts. Your emotions will lie.

⊱─────❀─────⊰

You will have disaster in your life. How long the trouble lasts, and how badly you are hurt will be up to you.

⊱─────❀─────⊰

The more adversity a deer faces, the greater his chances of survival are, and the same is for men. Adversity strengthens and sharpens the survival skills of both deer and men.

———————

Don't fear death, since it will happen. Instead, charge into life, and scare the fear of death away.

———————

Life is one great adventure with death being the greatest adventure of all.

———————

Pain is an opportunity to test and find endurance.

———————

There are three kinds of problems in life:

1. Things you can change - try to change them immediately.

2. Things only time can change - learn patience.

3. Things that can't be changed - forget them.

───────✦───────

Life is the greatest adventure you'll ever have. Don't waste it.

───────✦───────

If you fear losing your life, you'll never really live.

───────✦───────

The eagle that fears to fall never will learn to fly.

───────✦───────

By bending with the wind, the mighty oak stands the test of time and isn't pushed around by most winds.

The butterfly is not the only living thing that lives in a world of constant change.

A mistake is what you make of it. A disaster is a blessing in disguise.

One knocking down is worth two tellings.

Every squirrel is responsible for its life and the amount of nuts it stores every year.

Unhappiness may occur when someone doesn't realize how well off he is.

Those who don't follow a dream follow nothing
and become the same.

When your life is at its worse, help someone
else, and your own problems will diminish.

A man's life should not be summed up in the
way he lives or how he dies, but by the influence
he leaves on those he's known. That's where the
good or evil of a man's life remains.

A man who knows not God knows neither life
nor death.

What have all men in all times always searched for - oneness with God.

The biggest fear of most people is the fear of being alone. Learn to spend time alone now, and you won't fear it later.

God spoke through a jackass in Acts 9 when he spoke to Saul of Tarsus on the road to Damascus. Do you think he can't speak through you or use you? He can.

Thoughts on Love

Falling in love is no reason to marry, because you can fall in love with anything - Oreo cookies, a canary, a goldfish or even a peanut-butter-and-jelly sandwich.

If you're looking for a mate, find a friend first. Love will come later.

When you get a divorce, you're gambling that the new mate you find will be better than the one you've lost. However, the odds are against you.

If nobody loves you, then find somebody to love.

⟡⟡⟡⟡⟡⟡⟡⟡

Happiness, when given away, can multiply faster than rabbits.

⟡⟡⟡⟡⟡⟡⟡⟡

The only way to win at love is not to be afraid to love.

⟡⟡⟡⟡⟡⟡⟡⟡

Love is giving.

⟡⟡⟡⟡⟡⟡⟡⟡

Hurt feelings are worse than a punch in the nose. Healed feelings are better than a cold drink of water on a hot day.

⟡⟡⟡⟡⟡⟡⟡⟡

Lasting love is not dependent and should not be concerned with the good qualities you see in someone. Lasting love is dependent on your ability and willingness to endure the things you don't like about someone.

When someone doesn't love you, they may have failed to realize what they are missing.

Love may hurt more often than it feels good.

If you don't genuinely love someone, don't give them any advice, or else you only may be trying to manipulate them.

Thoughts on Men and Women

There is no such thing as a self-made man.
Wise men know this and give credit where
credit is due.

I'd rather get in a fist fight than listen to a
woman gripe.

The only effective tool to break a bad habit is
the human will.

A man without God has nothing.

I'd rather get kicked in the face by a wild horse than listen to a nagging woman.

———————————

The beauty in a woman won't be seen in the paint on the outside but in the character on the inside.

———————————

I don't understand why men will believe a fish they can't see will bite a hook and not believe there is a God.

———————————

Every man is only a boy with gray hair.

———————————

The easiest way for a woman to get what she wants from most men is to play the game of "damsel in distress."

Dogs, deer and men face the most danger during the breeding season.

Thoughts on Money

The most-sound investment is in your own abilities.

Rich is a man who can pay all his bills at the end of the month when they come due.

The more problems you can solve, the more money you will make.

I'd rather go broke testing a good idea then let a good idea go untested.

Invest in people rather than banks. Then when the banks close with all your money, you can go to the people you've invested in, and they will give you something to eat.

If you act unusual, you're considered weird if you're poor but eccentric if you're rich.

If your goal in life is not to have money, give yours to me.

Three things money can't buy are poverty, a sound mind and happiness.

Remember, even if you go broke, the government still will feed you, clothe you and take care of you when you are sick.

Thoughts on Money

———————✦———————

There are millions to be made in any occupation, even collecting garbage.

———————✦———————

The more people you try to make rich, the more folks who will be working to try to make you rich.

———————✦———————

The more money you give out, the more dollars that will be returned to you.

———————✦———————

The more you give away, the more you'll have.

———————✦———————

You will become the most creative when you are broke.

The richest life is where learning and wonder never cease.

Easy money has no value.

Enough is just a little bit more than you have.

There are two ways to make a lot of money - work hard and learn as you go or learn from the mistakes of others. The most money you ever will make is what you save.

Within every misfortune are the seeds for great fortune.

Often the difference in a person becoming an intelligent millionaire is simply having another person say, "You can."

Buying people's brains are the best investment of any business.

Your money is your money and not your children's money. If they want money, let them earn it like you have. Then they always will know how to get it.

The secret of wealth is systematically investing in your future and the futures of others.

Anyone can earn money, but can you keep it and grow it? That's the real challenge.

The Briar Patch Philosopher

Thoughts on People

The happiest person in life is the one who doesn't fear death.

The more people who know your personal business, the less business you will have.

A friend still loves you - even if you're wrong.

The biggest problem in business is people understanding people.

The most-courageous men and women I ever knew never fought a war or stood in the face of a charging train. Instead they faced life's greatest fears and pain without a whimper or a complaint.

What makes a man rich or poor - money, fame, riches or power? None of these! His thoughts and views of himself - that's where he finds life's poverty or riches.

A friend is someone who doesn't punch you in the nose, even though you've got it coming.

A good deed never returns empty-handed.

Character is what you are when nobody's looking.

When people are talking about you, at least they're not gossiping about someone else.

A mad dog often bites himself first, and usually your anger hurts you more than it does others.

Don't be too disappointed in people. Even Jesus had a few rats in his pack.

Remember, dead folks are the only people who don't have problems.

There are two kinds of people in life - happy and sad. Happy people don't stay sad long, and sad people seldom stay happy long.

※※※※※※※※※※※※

Even the meanest folks need a soft touch.

※※※※※※※※※※※※

The meanest person you ever will meet is the tongue in your own mouth.

※※※※※※※※※※※※

Everyone you meet is the world's greatest something. Find out what that something is, and you will discover a gold mine for you and them.

※※※※※※※※※※※※

Be kind to old people, because you're destined to become one.

※※※※※※※※※※※※

Many times if you tell someone they can, they will.

Churches and prisons - you may find the same kinds of people in both.

Those who look down on others never can look up to see a better world.

The brave are those who choose to face fear.

Often the difference in a hero and a coward is the amount of time they take to face a problem.

Those who coast through life never climb the mountains and see the Promised Land.

Life ain't easy. Anyone who tells you it is will lie about something else.

The noblest buck in the forest not only fights the most but also suffers the most.

Be different. There are enough ordinary people in the world. You don't have to grow up. You only may be required to play slower.

Everyone has hardships. Some people just seem to enjoy talking about them more than others.

Disease, anger and hatred are all carried by sick people. Happiness is carried by well people.

Who's to say that a mentally-challenged person is not in a better world than we are.

Good employees are created, not hired.

Thoughts on Success

Four Reasons People Fail - They:

- are lazy;
- won't learn and continue to learn;
- believe what other people say instead of what they know; and
- lack a passion for success.

A successful life is when your children are better people than you.

The fastest way from where you are to where you want to be is in your ability to choose the right mentors and your ability to follow their leads.

Your success only can grow as big as you dream.

What would you do with a billion dollars? As you answer this question, you'll discover who you are, and what you are.

Freedom is within your grasp if you only will jump and grab for it.

Wealth is mental, not physical.

When you fail, you really have succeeded. Then you know what won't work and can begin again to find out what will.

Great things only come to those who dream great dreams.

Attack your fears. What you fear most, do first.

Often the difference in winning and losing the race is not how fast you run but how long you run.

All the dogs in the back of the pack yap at the leader.

Successful people never quit. Losers never start.

Losing is not final as long as you realize that sooner or later you will win if you keep trying.

Listen to your inner voice, which often defies reason. If you follow that voice, it will lead you to greatness.

Most great men and women have been thought to be nuts at some time in their lives.

Don't be a slave to your failures. Begin new successes immediately.

Only through the fires of tribulation can your mettle be tested.

An education doesn't give you more tools to work with; it just sharpens the tools you already have.

You can't beat a man who won't quit.

Opportunity is around us every day. Smart people look for opportunity and take advantage of it. Average people avoid opportunity by saying, "I don't think I can do it," or worrying, "What if I fail?"

The most-successful people in life are the ones who fail the most and learn from their failures.

All are born for greatness. Some find it. Most never look.

⟆⟆⟆⟆⟆⟆⟆⟆⟆⟆

"But they that wait upon the Lord shall renew their strength; they shall mount up with wings as eagles; they shall run, and not be weary; and they shall walk, and not faint." Isaiah 41:31

⟆⟆⟆⟆⟆⟆⟆⟆⟆⟆

Often the door we want has to close, so the door we need can open.

⟆⟆⟆⟆⟆⟆⟆⟆⟆⟆

"Where does the power come from to see the race to its end? From within." - the movie, "Chariots of Fire"

⟆⟆⟆⟆⟆⟆⟆⟆⟆⟆

No great accomplishment of man ever occurred without a great dream by an ordinary person.

The only dog in the pack whose view ever changes is the leader.

You either have to get down on the ground and fight for your food or lay on the porch and let the big dogs eat.

Continuing to fail until you reach success is better than taking the safe, sure route to mediocrity.

You can become only as great as your biggest dream.

The best blackberries in any patch are reserved for those willing to go through the most thorns.

Open every door of opportunity that's before you. Most of the time there will be a gorilla behind the door. You must slam it quickly. But every now and then, there is a pony that you can ride on to success. However, if you fail to open the doors, you never find the ponies.

When do you strike out in life? Only when you quit coming to bat. Successful people endure failure longer than unsuccessful people.

Failure is much-more important than success. Fear of failure prevents success.

What you're willing to give up often is more important than what you get.

Success is not measured by how many times you fall down, but how quickly you get up.

No success is fulfilling, unless in the process you make someone else successful also.

When the osprey (fish hawk) dives from the air into water he doesn't know, he may die. However, most often his courage is rewarded with a bountiful fish dinner.

Only those who fight deserve the victor's crown.

A leader is one who puts others' well-being ahead of his own.

When you run with dogs, you have to be sure you don't get their fleas.

All that's required to live the life of your dreams is the courage to try and the tenacity not to quit.

The kites that fly the highest must climb against the strongest winds.

There is no shame to falling or failing. The only shame is if you don't get up and move on.

Seldom does any one glory in another's success.

To be successful, choose successful friends, and learn from them.

Fear is required for success.

The sharpest of knives and people are honed against the hardest rocks.

Facing adversity and developing self-discipline are the keys to a successful life.

All young people are success stories. They simply need people to believe in them.

The quickest way to success is to find someone who is what you want to be and do what he or she tells you to do.

People fail for only one reason - they quit before they succeed.

Sleep is the enemy of the successful man.

Thoughts on Wisdom

Hummingbirds spend their lives looking for beauty and the sweet things of life. The buzzard spends its life looking for the dead, the corrupt and the stinking things of life. Which are you?

Work and study are the gas and the oil that fuel your dreams.

You choose whether to be happy or sad

Always keep cash money in your pocket to buy something to eat, dry socks on your feet to

Stay warm and a smile on your face to make people wonder what you've been up to.

***

The only true treasure we ever can store up is memories.

***

The greatest treasure in life is knowing the truth about yourself.

***

Life is a collection of memories and beliefs lived and hopefully passed on to others and your family

***

Wisdom comes from those who survive and learn from their mistakes.

***

Speak knowledge, and you never grow old.

Did you learn the most from a spanking or a gift?

Right does not always have to be politically correct.

If everyone else's children are doing something, yours probably shouldn't.

Embrace fear, because it is an excellent motivator

If you are waiting to decide what to do, do something while you're waiting.

※※※※※※※※※

Wisdom is all around us all the time, but you have to have wisdom to see it.

※※※※※※※※※

When you move into a new area, immediately find a doctor, a lawyer, a banker, a dentist and a preacher. You will need them all.

※※※※※※※※※

To hit the target, you must aim and shoot. Aiming alone will not produce the desired result.

※※※※※※※※※

A fitting epithet for us all - "A life well spent in the service of others." Will that be yours?

※※※※※※※※※

The shorter life gets, the more we see how much of it we have wasted.

⟐⟐⟐⟐⟐⟐⟐⟐⟐⟐

Happiness is one of the few things in life that the more you give away, the more you keep.

⟐⟐⟐⟐⟐⟐⟐⟐⟐⟐

If the airplane you're in exploded in the sky, what are five things you would want to say to five people you know? Say them now!

⟐⟐⟐⟐⟐⟐⟐⟐⟐⟐

Life is fun. If it's not, then there's something wrong with you. Find out what, and change it. You can!

⟐⟐⟐⟐⟐⟐⟐⟐⟐⟐

Life is a race. The beginning we can't control, and the end can't be determined. But how well we run in the middle is all that counts.

The real secret for a successful and happy life is not what you achieve in your lifetime, but what you help others achieve in theirs.

"Be the best you can be," my father told me. After more than 50 years, I finally realized this was a goal I never could achieve, but by constantly trying, I could become better every day.

You can find God in strange places if you look for Him. He often speaks to you through strange people in strange events. All you have to do is listen.

Ultimate truth: All men throughout all times have searched for ultimate truth. Few have found it. Many have learned that ultimate truth comes from making our lives a constant prayer to our creator and then listening for His direction.

***

Wisdom is the search for why and once found, sharing it with others.

***

Feelings change, but truth remains.

***

The real joy in life comes from your ability to derive joy from the success of others.

***

The body may age, but the mind should improve.

***

Every day my brother passed by an old man shoveling a mountain of coal. Each afternoon when he passed by that same man, the mountain of coal was gone. One day my brother asked, "How do you move that mountain of coal each day?" The man looked up and said, "One shovel of coal at a time." You too can move a mountain.

This too surely will pass.

Work out-competes brilliance every time.

Education comes from books and school, and books and school make learning easier.

You only know how precious life is when you face death.

Jesus is the only man who talks in red letters

There is good in every tragedy. Wisdom is being able to see that good and not just the tragedy.

Always listen to people who are smarter than you, and then make your own decisions.

You learn more from saying nothing than you do when you're trying to impart knowledge by talking.

Wisdom is realizing that often the window of hope must close, so the door of opportunity can open.

⊰••≺•≻•⊱

Doing right always is better than doing wrong.

⊰••≺•≻•⊱

Most wrong decisions are made quickly.

⊰••≺•≻•⊱

When you worry about the worst thing that can happen to you, remember there's a 90-percent chance it won't.

⊰••≺•≻•⊱

Learn not to share ignorance. If you don't know something, keep your mouth shut.

⊰••≺•≻•⊱

Learn to respond, not react.

The difference in a problem and an opportunity
often is your view of the situation.

If you can't believe in yourself, then believe in
what others think you can be.

The wisest man in the world asked for wisdom.
He knew that once wisdom was found,
everything he wanted would be easy to find.

Wisdom comes when we recognize the truth
about others.

"Any fool can make a rule, and every fool will mind it." - Thoreau

~~~~~~~~~~~~~~~

Wisdom often comes after your nose is smashed.

~~~~~~~~~~~~~~~

Participating in an argument is much like trying to teach a pig to sing. You waste your time and irritate the pig.

~~~~~~~~~~~~~~~

Solomon said it best when he said, "Ego, ego. All the world is one big ego trip." (loosely translated)

~~~~~~~~~~~~~~~

Think you're a genius? Well, remember genius rarely is recognized until the person is dead.

Worry is only believing the worst will happen. The truth is it rarely does.

Wisdom often is found in the most-ordinary places from the most-ordinary people.

The search for wisdom is the secret to a successful life. However, most of us start too late and learn too little.

Use the book of Proverbs from the Bible as a short course in wisdom.

Wisdom is a strange commodity. The more you get, the more you give away.

Wisdom comes from seeing why bad things happen to you and using disaster for your triumph.

When King Solomon, now known as the wisest man in the world, was asked by the God of the Universe what He should give Solomon, the King chose wisdom - which is the right answer to all questions.

Thoughts on Work

Find an occupation that's more fun than anything you've ever done in your life. If you try to build a business based on what's fun to you, then you'll never work a day in your life. You'll also feel that you're getting paid to play, even if you're putting in 60 or 100 hours a week

If I give my best effort and finish the race, I win.

Always run to win.

Two character traits that rarely ever walk in the same pair of shoes are creativity and organization.

~~~~~~~~~~~~~~~

Writing allows you to organize your thoughts and plan your future.

~~~~~~~~~~~~~~~

Work 12, 14 or 16 hours a day. Mediocre people work 40 hours a week. Successful people work 80 to 100 hours a week.

~~~~~~~~~~~~~~~

Procrastination is the death of a good idea.

~~~~~~~~~~~~~~~

When all else fails . . . charge.

~~~~~~~~~~~~~~~

While you're waiting on the Lord, let Him find you working.

An excess of work will make up for a lack of brains.

The man rowing the boat doesn't have time to worry about who's rocking it.

If you aren't being criticized, you probably aren't doing anything.

I can do today what most people won't, so I can live tomorrow like most people can't.

If you're in motion, stay in motion. If you rest, you may not start again.

There are two types of people - the people who work and the people who gripe about working.

The flip side of having too much work is unemployment.

No product has value until a salesman sells it.

If a company doesn't have a problem for you to solve, then you don't have a job.

Work doesn't have to be miserable to be profitable. Take a job doing what you like; the money will follow.

⁓⁓⁓⁓⁓⁓⁓⁓⁓

A job worth doing is worth doing right.

⁓⁓⁓⁓⁓⁓⁓⁓⁓

In business as well as in life, the more you grease the wheels, the faster and better they'll roll.

⁓⁓⁓⁓⁓⁓⁓⁓⁓

Creativity is a daydream tried.

⁓⁓⁓⁓⁓⁓⁓⁓⁓

If you strive to make everyone who works for you or with you successful, you never will fail.

⁓⁓⁓⁓⁓⁓⁓⁓⁓

There's always is a job for a man who will work.

There is no good or bad work. Work is work, and only attitude determines the way you feel about it.

Even a watermelon has seeds that must be spit out before you can swallow the sweet red treat.

To be successful, don't dodge problems. Hunt problems to solve. Problem solvers get rich. Those who dodge problems get fired.

Your best chance to make it is to out-work all those who don't.

Work like a non-union beaver.

The only time you can't work is when you're brain-dead. If you can communicate, you can earn a living.

The greatest people in any profession aren't necessarily the smartest or the quickest. They are the ones who won't quit and never have accepted defeat as final.

Freelance writing is the only profession I know of where the less you know, the more you can learn, and the more you can make.

Fear is the greatest ally of a freelancer.

You can't catch a fox that won't quit running, and your creditors never will overtake you as long as you keep on working.

Thoughts on Politics

Politics is a game made for compromise. Players of the game don't do what they want to do; they do what they can.

A politician tells you what he and the government will do for you. A statesman tells you what he's going to prevent the government from doing to you.

There is no political party as strong as one man dedicated to a single purpose.

When you mount your white horse, don't forget the mud will show up more.

In politics when someone walks like a duck, talks like a duck and has webbed feet, but claims to be a peacock, well, you know he's all wet... and is probably a duck.

A Conversation with the Author John E. Phillips

Question: John, why did you write "The Briar Patch Philosopher?"

Phillips: Since my idealistic college days, I've been a seeker of knowledge, wisdom and truth. I learned that when I found morsels of any of these that I needed to write them down and save them. However, I lost the opportunity to mine one of the greatest storehouses of each of these virtues when my father passed away. I had a brilliant plan at that time. I just had bought the latest and greatest reel-to-reel tape recorder. My dad had come home that day from the hospital after more stays in the hospital than I could count. Diabetes, heart trouble and generally worn-out from years of hard work had ruined my dad's health. My dad knew, as I did, that he wouldn't be in this world much longer. So, on Pop's first night at home, I plugged in the tape recorder and asked him to record his sayings as well as the wisdom he had shared with me, my brother and my sister for so many years and the many things he thought were important for us to know and remember. I asked him to count into the microphone of the tape recorder. He counted to 10, I replayed the recording, and I was confident that all he had to do was push a button to record his wisdom, knowledge and the truths he had learned in his life and had passed on to us. I left Pop's house at 9:00 pm and went home. At 1:00 am, I got the call, "Your dad is gone." I had lost my best chance to get some of the best information for this book that I ever had had. Over the last 20+ years, I've tried to remember many of his sayings, and the ideas he taught his family and write his words down. I've also collected wisdom wherever I've found it. We all have opportunities to collect and store wisdom every day. If we miss those chances, they never may come again.

Question: John, where did you get all these sayings and gems of wisdom?

Phillips: Many of these sayings have come from my family, friends, Sunday School teachers, preachers, tenant farmers, mechanics, plumbers, welders and businessmen.

Question: Why do you think these sayings are so important?

Phillips: Many of these sayings govern our lives. My dad once told me, "Son, I'd be proud of you, even if you were a garbage collector, as long as you were the best garbage collector ever." I learned then that striving to be the best often is reaching for an impossible goal. And, in that quest to be the best, you become far more than you've ever thought you can be. So, little sayings can have a powerful impact on our lives, if we can recognize the wisdom in them.

Question: Why do you think wisdom is so important?

Phillips: Wisdom thinks first, speaks second and acts last. If we think before we speak, and if we invoke wisdom before we act, we'll almost always make the right choices in our lives. Life is a series of choices. Those who make the best choices have the happiest, most-successful lives and receive the greatest rewards in the lives of their children. Fools demonstrate a lack of wisdom and a disregard of its value. I want a better life, so I want to learn all I can from everyone I can about how to make right choices.

Question: John, what do you want the reader to know about you from this book?

Phillips: The greatest rewards I seek from this book aren't money or fame but rather that someone reads these words, and hopefully these words change that person's life for the better. For what more can a humble scribe hope? "Wisdom is the principal thing; therefore get wisdom; and with all your getting, get understanding." Proverbs 4: 7, "The Holy Bible"

Dedication

"Pop, you're burning the candle at both ends," I told my dad with concern years ago. "If you don't slow down, you're going to burn out." But my dad, who never passed-up a chance to double-over at work - work two, 8-hour shifts back to back - said, "I can burn the candle at both ends. All I need is a little more wax in the middle. I know I've only got one candle to burn in this life, and I want to burn the flame as high and as bright for as long as I can. Once the candle goes out, it'll be out for a long time."

W.A. Phillips, Sr., was the hardest-working man I ever met. At one time, even after having had three heart attacks before the age of 40, he worked his regular shifts at U.S. Steel as a mixing operator, he built a restaurant he named Phillips' Pantry that he and my mother ran 6-½-days a week, he also owned and maintained more than 20 rental houses, and he invested heavily in the stock market. He had a business plan that worked. Any money he made from working overtime was the money he used to invest.

One time U.S. Steel offered their older employees 13 weeks of paid vacation, but my dad only took 2 weeks. When I asked him why, he smiled and answered, "If those folks at U.S. Steel find out they don't need me to work for 13 weeks, they may decide that they don't need me to work at all. During those 11 weeks I'm working instead of being on vacation, I can earn twice as much as I do at any other time of the year."

My dad generated, captured and preserved many of the truisms you'll find in this book. So, even though Pop has graduated from this life into another, I've tried to preserve some of his many sayings. This book is dedicated to the memory of William Archie Phillips, Sr.

About the Author

For the past 40 years, John E. Phillips of Vestavia, Alabama, has been a fulltime outdoor writer, traveling the world interviewing hunters, guides, outfitters and other outdoorsmen about how they hunt. An award-winning author, John has been hunting and fishing since his kindergarten days with his dad and brother and has had the good fortune to fish and hunt with experts. He's also travelled across the U.S. as a newspaper writer, magazine writer, outdoor photographer and radio host, and for the last 13 years, as a provider of outdoors internet content for numerous companies daily. He was the 2007 Legendary Communicator chosen for induction into the National Fresh Water Hall of Fame, the Crossbow Communicator of the Year in 2008,

and in 2012, he was presented the Homer Circle Fishing Communicator Award by the American Sportfishing Association and the Professional Outdoor Media Association. To learn more the author and his life experiences, go to http://nighthawkpublications.com/Bio%20Page/john.htm.

You can visit John's Amazon author page at www.amazon.com/author/johnephillips.

Other Books by John E. Phillips

For more information about these Kindle ebooks, go to www.amazon.com/kindle, type John E. Phillips into Search and click on Author's Page (2nd choice) when it comes up to see books available.

The 10 Sins of Turkey Hunting with Preston Pittman

13 Breakfast Recipes You Can't Live Without

13 Chili Recipes You Can't Live Without

13 Deer Recipes You Can't Live Without

13 Freshwater Fish Recipes You Can't Live Without

13 Saltwater Fish Recipes You Can't Live Without

13 Seafood Recipes You Can't Live Without

13 Soup, Chowder and Gumbo Recipes You Can't Live Without

13 Stew Recipes You Can't Live Without

13 Wild Turkey Recipes You Can't Live Without

Alabama's Inshore Saltwater Fishing: A Year-Round Guide for Catching More Than 15 Species

Alabama's Offshore Saltwater Fishing: A Year-Round Guide for Catching Over 15 Species of Fish

America's Greatest Bass Fisherman

The Best Wild Game & Seafood Cookbook Ever: 350 Southern Recipes for Deer, Turkey, Fish, Seafood, Small Game and Birds

Bowhunting Deer: The Secrets of the PSE Pros

Bowhunting the Dangerous Bears of Alaska

Catching Speckled Trout and Redfish: Learn from Alabama's Best Fishermen

Catch the Most and Biggest Bass in Any Lake: 18 Pro Fishermen's Best Tactics

Catfish Like a Pro

Courage: Stories of Hometown Heroes

Crappie: How to Catch them Spring and Summer

Deer & Fixings: How to Cook Delicious Venison

For Hot-Weather Fishing Success, Head to Reelfoot

Fishing Mississippi's Gulf Coast and Visitor's Guide

Hot-Weather Bass Tactics

How to Bass Fish Like a Pro

How to Become a Tournament Bass Fisherman

How to Find Your Elk and Get Him in Close

How to Fish Mississippi's Gulf Coast in June

How to Hunt Deer Like a Pro

How to Hunt Deer Up Close: With Bows, Rifles, Muzzleloaders and Crossbows

How to Hunt Turkeys with World Champion Preston Pittman

How to Make Money with Taxidermy: 70 Tips for Hunters and Small Businesses

How to Win a Bass Tournament: Personal Lessons from 8 Pro Bass Fishermen

Jim Crumley's Secrets of Bowhunting Deer

The John E. Phillips Sampler: Hunting, Fishing and More

The Most Dangerous Game with a Bow: Secrets of the PSE Pros

Moving Forward: Stories of Hometown Heroes

Outdoor Life's Complete Turkey Hunting

PhD Elk: How to Hunt the Smartest Elk in Any State

PhD Gobblers: How to Hunt the Smartest Turkeys in the World

PhD Whitetails: How to Hunt and Take the Smartest Deer on Any Property

The Recipes You Can't Live Without

The Recipes You Can't Live Without: Chilis, Stews, Soups, Chowders & Gumbo

The Recipes You Can't Live Without: Freshwater & Saltwater Fish & Seafood

Reelfoot Lake: How to Fish for Crappie, Bass, Bluegills and Catfish and Hunt for Ducks

Secrets for Catching Red Snapper and Grouper in the Gulf of Mexico

Secrets for Hunting Elk
The Turkey Hunter's Bible
Turkey Hunting Tactics

To buy my print books on hunting, visit: http://nighthawkpublications.com/hunting/hunting.htm. These books include:

"Black Powder Hunting Secrets"

"Complete Turkey Hunting"

"Deer & Fixings"

"How to Take Monster Bucks"

"Jim Crumley's Secrets of Bowhunting Deer"

"The Masters' Secrets of Bowhunting Deer"

"The Masters' Secrets of Deer Hunting"

"The Masters' Secrets of Turkey Hunting"

"PhD Gobblers"

"PhD Whitetails"

"The Science of Deer Hunting"

"Turkey Hunting Tactics"

For my fishing books, go to http://nighthawkpublications.com/fishing/fishing.htm. These books include:

"Bass Fishing Central Alabama"

"Fish & Fixings"

"Masters' Secrets of Catfishing"

"Masters' Secrets of Crappie Fishing"

Go to www.amazon.com and type in the names of our other print books to view them:

The Turkey Hunter's Bible

Crappie: How to Catch Them Spring and Summer

Thank you for reading "The Briar Patch Philosopher." If you enjoyed this book, please let us know by leaving a review on Amazon.

www.ingramcontent.com/pod-product-compliance
Lightning Source LLC
Chambersburg PA
CBHW070545030426
42337CB00016B/2363